Delegation

Brian Rothwell

DIRECTORY OF SOCIAL CHANGE

Published by
Directory of Social Change
24 Stephenson Way
London NW1 2DP
Tel. 08450 77 77 07; Fax 020 7391 4804
email publications@dsc.org.uk
www.dsc.org.uk
from whom further copies and a full books catalogue are available.

Directory of Social Change is a Registered Charity no. 800517

First published 2009

ISBN 978 1 906294 11 3

British Library Cataloguing in Publication Data

A catalogue record for this book is available from the British Library

Cover and text designed by Kate Bass
Typeset by Marlinzo Services, Frome
Printed and bound by Martins of Berwick

All Directory of Social Change departments in London:
08450 77 77 07

Directory of Social Change Northern Office:
Research 0151 708 0136

Contents

Introduction

Who will this book help?

Delegation is not easy. Nearly everyone is in favour of it as an abstract concept, rather like the majority of the population would agree with other abstract concepts such as justice and freedom. However, delegation in real life requires effort and perseverance in the face of discouragement and disappointment. It doesn't work all of the time.

This practical guide will help all managers who are responsible for the performance of others. In particular it will aid individuals who are new to management and develop the skills of managers who are unused to delegating and those who recognise that they have a problem with the concept.

What will it give you?

This book provides guidance on how to make sure that delegation works well and, as a result, should help you enjoy greater managerial satisfaction. Sticking to these guidelines will allow you to get a job done more efficiently, your time will be freed up to focus on the more important aspects of your job and it will enable you to develop members of staff.

The manager who fails to delegate is not a real manager. The manager who delegates has made a start on the road to becoming exceptional at their chosen job.

Chapter 1

What is delegation?

This chapter looks at what delegation is and is not, and the risks and benefits involved in delegating.

Delegation is one of the most important aspects of any manager's job. It is an area where managers frequently have great freedom of choice because what they choose to delegate, to whom and when, is almost entirely at their own discretion.

All members of staff have their own duties. They have their own jobs to do – and so do managers. Delegation is not about allocating the work that naturally falls into the duties of staff members. Managers may have to decide who handles which piece of work, and that may depend on the balance of individual workloads within a department. However, this is not delegation.

Delegation is when a manager deliberately chooses to give a reporting staff member the authority to undertake a piece of work that is normally handled at managerial level. It requires a modicum of courage, a degree of patience and no small amount of judgement.

Top tip

Be a gardener at work. Grow people.

Julia Cleverdon, CEO, Business in the Community

Three important distinctions

In defining delegation, it is important to make three distinctions. First, 'responsibility' in this context means the work that is to be delegated – the project, task, job or duty. Second, 'authority' means the power or the right to make decisions and take action to enable a responsibility to be handed over. Traffic wardens have the responsibility to prevent vehicles from obstructing other road users. They need the authority to issue parking tickets. Without this authority their job cannot be done. Delegation always involves matching the responsibility with the appropriate authority.

Third, is the distinction of what *cannot* be delegated. This is the manager's accountability for the totality of what goes on in the department or team. You can delegate a responsibility by ensuring that you give the member of staff the right level of authority to carry it out. But accountability for the performance of the task delegated remains with you, as the manager making the decision to delegate.

You can have a one-to-one conversation with a member of staff about a delegated responsibility that has been handled badly, but in front of anyone else – whether they are from inside or outside the organisation – you cannot shirk your accountability for the performance of the delegated task. It is the manager who must face the wrath of annoyed clients or irate members of staff from other departments. And this is logical because it was the manager who made the decision to delegate the job concerned.

It is this third aspect of delegation that involves you taking the calculated risk that a member of staff will do the delegated job as well as needs to be done to satisfy the rest of the internal organisation or the external client.

Top tip

Being publicly accountable for the work that you delegate can be a scary thought. But don't let it put you off! The benefits of delegating far outweigh any problems you may encounter.

The benefits of delegating

The risks of delegating are counterbalanced by a number of potential benefits. These are so great that if you fail to delegate you are throwing away a number of significant opportunities.

■ **Delegation frees up a manager's time and enables them to focus on the really important aspects of their job.** This is vital to the job satisfaction of any manager. Time spent on the duties that require your personal knowledge, skill and experience is much more satisfying and stretching than time spent on jobs that could be delegated.

■ **Any manager's job should be about planning the future as well as about organising the present.** It should also be about focusing on outside events that might have a bearing on the performance of the department or team. Delegation enables you to find the time to plan for the future, anticipate necessary change and stay one step ahead of the competition.

■ **Managers who delegate well are likely to have staff who think of them as good bosses.** Delegation does wonders for staff morale. Employees who are being developed and who grow in their jobs by being given opportunities to learn new skills are always happier at work than those who are not. Happier staff are much more likely to have low levels of absenteeism, indulge in less office politics and be more prepared to work late when the pressure is on.

■ **Effective delegation ensures that work is carried out at the most relevant level in the organisation.** Not only is this more efficient because people earning smaller salaries carry out the delegated jobs but also it means that decisions are made by staff who are closer to the end-user or beneficiary than the manager. Decisions made by people close to the end-user are more likely to be right, and the resulting actions are more likely to be carried out

Top tip

Spend some time thinking about what sorts of things you could be doing if you delegated more and how much time you could free up. This should help motivate you to delegate.

with enthusiasm. Good delegation creates jobs that people are enthusiastic about because they involve responsibilities that allow staff to make their own decisions.

■ **Delegation is the best possible way of preparing staff for greater responsibilities within the department.** All managers will need someone to undertake a new departmental task, or exploit a new opportunity at some point. Individuals who have been developed through continual delegation are a much better bet in these circumstances than those who have to be shoehorned into an unfamiliar role.

■ **Delegation is the best way of producing staff worthy of promotion outside the department.** They may move on to greater responsibilities either inside or outside the organisation, but the satisfaction derived from their development and promotion will more than compensate for their loss.

■ **A manager who has delegated well has a better chance of being promoted because there will be staff available to fill the vacancy that they would leave behind.** A manager who is immersed entirely in the detail of their job is less likely to be promoted. This is because it is very difficult to disentangle this sort of manager from their role.

The difficulties of delegating

Risk

All delegation involves risk. The person to whom you delegate may make a mess of their new duty and you may have to take valuable time to sort it out. This risk goes with the territory and must be accepted.

The risk can be minimised: firstly, by planning the delegation process carefully (see chapters 2 and 3) and secondly, by showing the member of staff that you have faith in their ability. A simple statement to the effect that you have confidence in the staff member's ability to do the job could prove the difference

Top tip

Delegate your managerial responsibilities, including your decision-making authority, to one member of staff while you are on leave: you have a much better chance of returning to a work place of calm effectiveness.

Debra Allcock Tyler, Chief Executive, DSC

between a delegated duty being performed well and a responsibility that is botched.

Loss of enjoyment

Some managers cannot bear to delegate the jobs they enjoy doing, even when the duties they retain are not central to getting the results that matter most. They think that they would be depriving themselves of part of the reason for doing their job in the first place. You should avoid this type of thinking.

To delegate well you must give up:

- the satisfaction of doing some of the things you normally do
- some of the things that keep you in control
- some of the things that you enjoy doing.

Fear of not looking busy

Most managers do not take enough time out at work to think. They do not like the thought that their team members may catch sight of them staring into space, seemingly doing very little. They use this as an excuse not to delegate – all because they like to be seen to look busy doing stuff. This is another temptation that has to be resisted.

The main job of a manager is to think. The head of a team or a department has to come up with ways to improve both current performance and future chances of success. Taking time out to think is vital and when a manager is doing this, they are busier than at any other time. Delegation gives managers much-needed time at work to think.

Loss of control

Some managers are reluctant to delegate because they like to feel that they are on top of all the details

Case study

The managing director of an insurance broking operation eventually recognised that he did not need to record and tally the insurance commissions as they came into the office, even if he did gain great satisfaction from the task. The job was allocated to an accounts clerk, who did the job just as well, leaving the MD to do tasks more central to his job such as developing new sources of business.

relating to their department. As a result, they take all important decisions and require frequent detailed reports, checks and data from their team members.

A better approach is to delegate as much as possible and then keep in touch with the work of the department by:

- walking the job
- doing spot checks
- regularly reviewing the progress of delegated work with staff members.

This way staff are more likely to be motivated and the department will perform better.

Risk of losing staff

Other managers refuse to delegate because they don't want to run the risk of losing good quality staff. They fear that developing people will result in losing them to other departments or through promotion elsewhere. In fact the reverse is true. Managers are much more likely to lose staff whom they refuse to develop because they are more likely to become de-motivated or bored by not being stretched in their current jobs.

Fears about quality

Perhaps the greatest hindrance to the delegation process is the entirely natural feeling that someone else won't do the job as well, or in the same way, as you do. However, this is just another excuse not to delegate. A member of staff may not do the job as well as you the first time they are asked to perform it, but over time and with the correct coaching performance will improve.

It is important to make the distinction that a job done differently from the way the manager has always done

Top tip

Walking the job – literally walking about your department so that you can see and be seen – gives you the opportunity to observe things in action and to ask questions. Most importantly it allows staff the chance to 'nobble' you if they have something they want to ask.

Debra Allcock Tyler, Chief Executive, DSC

it is not necessarily a job done badly. If the result is in line with expectations, the way that it is done should not matter.

Delayed results

The process of delegation is slow to produce results in the early stages. In the short term you may become busier by delegating because you will be adding the coaching of staff (see chapter 4) to your current workload. You need to be patient and not expect results to appear immediately. Improvements in performance will come over time.

Avoid using the twin excuses that you won't achieve short-term results or that you don't have the time to coach staff as reasons not to delegate.

Top tip

Try not to let the problem of being short on time put you off delegating. Anticipate the need for the work and decide how it can be done before you become trapped into doing to yourself.

Mike Hudson, Founder and Director, Compass Partnership

Chapter 2

How to delegate

This chapter looks at the practical aspects of delegation: what (and what not) to delegate, to whom and how.

Should you be delegating more?

Delegation checklist

- ❏ I work longer hours than my staff.
- ❏ I take work home almost every night.
- ❏ I am frequently interrupted at work by staff coming to me with questions, for advice or for decisions.
- ❏ I spend time at work doing things that others could do for themselves.
- ❏ I have unfinished jobs accumulating.
- ❏ I have difficulty meeting deadlines.
- ❏ I fail to take enough time out at work to think.
- ❏ I don't spend enough time on planning the future and managing the present.
- ❏ I feel that the morale of my staff could be improved.
- ❏ I do some jobs because I enjoy doing them, even though others could do the job just as well.
- ❏ Decisions could be taken at a more relevant section of my department.
- ❏ I lack confidence in my staff's abilities to take on more responsibility.

❏ I am short of staff who could potentially take on new departmental tasks.

❏ Staff members are leaving because they are not being developed and stretched.

❏ I believe that managers should always look busy in order to justify their salaries.

❏ I neglect to ask staff for their ideas about problems that arise in their work.

If the honest answer to any one of the sixteen questions is yes, then you need to be delegating more to your staff.

In the unlikely event that you honestly ticked no boxes, please read no further and apply for a promotion immediately.

Deciding what to delegate

Should you be delegating more?

All managers need a starting point to help them judge whether they could be delegating more. There are three ways to do this. They do not have to be carried out sequentially; they can be mixed and matched.

1   The simple questionnaire checklist above comprises a delegation health check. By looking at which of the statements you ticked, you can work out some of the symptoms and causes of your under-delegation.

2   You should analyse how you spend your time. The time you spend on your job activities should, by definition, reflect what is outlined in your job description (assuming it is up to date).

The easiest way of establishing how much time you actually spend is to review your diary over the last month or the last quarter, and jot down roughly how long you estimate was spent on each diary entry. Simple addition will reveal a pattern of what you have actually done.

Top tip

If you ask the person to whom you are delegating whether they understand what you've asked them to do, they will probably say yes, even if they don't have a clue! (It's difficult to admit otherwise.) To ensure comprehension, ask them to re-explain your instructions to you – that way you will know if there is any element that you need to explain more clearly.

Jamie Wilcox, Chief Executive, Volunteer Centre Kensington and Chelsea

3 Draw up a chart that reflects the objectives of the job and the activities undertaken:

Job objective/activity	Hours per time period	% of total	+ Too much 0 About right − Not enough	Delegation possibility YES/NO	Activity to delegate
Forward planning					
Customer liaison					
Budget					
Cost control					
Financial reporting					
Fundraising					
Visiting other departments					
Telephone calls					
Meetings					
Appraisal					
Staff training					
Etc.					

Case study

In 1940 the Enigma code of the Italian Navy was broken by a 19-year-old junior at Bletchley Park called Mavis Lever. She disregarded all the ways that codes had been cracked beforehand and invented her own solution.

What could you delegate?

In assessing the delegation potential of all the things that a manager gets involved in, there are three areas to examine for delegation potential. First, those tasks consuming a lot of time; second, the jobs that are urgent but not so important; and third, those activities which are important and routine at managerial level but may not be to a member of staff.

1 **Tasks that consume a lot of your time.** These provide obvious delegation opportunities. This is particularly so if you are not very proficient or have run out of new ways of tackling the tasks. A managerial request to produce a better and quicker way of solving a recurring problem may well become an irresistible challenge to a member of staff.

2   **As many tasks as possible that are of low importance.** All managerial activities can be categorised into issues that are of lower or higher importance. They can also be categorised into urgent or non-urgent items. One secret of success in management is to concentrate on the things that are important before they become urgent.

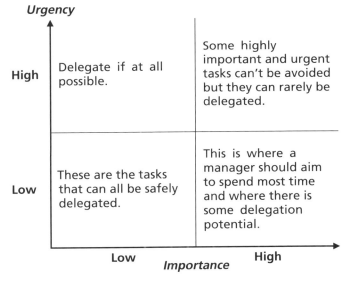

Urgency

	Low	High
High	Delegate if at all possible.	Some highly important and urgent tasks can't be avoided but they can rarely be delegated.
Low	These are the tasks that can all be safely delegated.	This is where a manager should aim to spend most time and where there is some delegation potential.

Importance

3   **Routine important tasks.** The departmental monthly financial return falls into the 'important' category in that it has to be done accurately and submitted on time. However, there is no need for you to complete it. You may need to sign it off but there is no need to spend time working on it at a detailed level.

What is routine to you will be new to the member of staff and, by delegating the activity, you can both stretch and develop them and free up more of your time – time that you should be spending on getting the results that managers are paid to achieve.

Case study

One company secretary finally accepted that the right time to write the minutes of the board meeting was straight afterwards. The wrong time to write them was in a panic a week before the next meeting when prompted that the agenda for the next meeting needed to be sent out.

Acting the right way, he prevented an important task becoming urgent.

Essential don'ts in planning to delegate

There are three limitations that should immediately narrow your choice if you wish to delegate more. These must be recognised and deleted from any list of possible planned delegation activities even if there is a staff member itching to take on more work.

Top tip

If the task is not normally handled at managerial level nor is it a chance for development, present it as a favour. If you disguise it as a delegation opportunity it will most likely cause resentment, especially if the person feels obliged to do it.

- **Responsibilities for confidential, security or policy matters that are restricted to managerial level**. If there is an organisational rule that restricts a responsibility to a senior level, the rule must be respected. You have the right to try to get the rule changed by appealing to more senior colleagues or the board of trustees. However, as long as it exists you should acknowledge and obey it.

- **Matters involving the exercise of discipline within your department**. It is logical that a staff member cannot be made responsible for disciplining colleagues who are their peers. This responsibility has to be retained by the manager.

- **Tasks that are well beyond the skills and experience of the staff member concerned.** Delegating to a junior colleague who has neither the skills nor the experience to do the delegated activity is akin to setting someone up to fail. If you do this deliberately or through a lack of thought, it is extremely unlikely that your team member will trust you again.

It is different if the staff member has the skill but not the experience. In this situation, careful coaching could produce the required delegated result.

Delegating responsibly

When you have identified certain tasks that can be delegated, you then have to decide to whom, and how, the jobs should be allocated.

The whole purpose of delegation is to give an individual an additional responsibility with the authority to carry it through. If you give the same responsibility to a team of people and give them all the authority to produce a result, it will end in chaos. One consequence of this folly is that some staff may decide to compete with each other to be first or to do the best job. At best this is a duplication of work by scarce resources, at worst it will lead to internal bickering. Another more likely consequence is that everyone will assume that someone else is responsible and that nothing will be done at all.

To whom should you delegate?

Deciding who should be given the task involves analysing each member of staff in turn, thinking through the following questions.

- What skills, qualifications and experience does the person have:
  - that are currently being used?
  - that are not being used in their job?
- What type of work has the individual shown interest in but has not yet done?
- What type of work would be unfair to expect an individual to do no matter how much training and coaching they receive?

The answers to these questions and reference to appraisal interviews should help to indicate who could be approached.

Top tip

Always delegate to an individual, never to a group of people or a team.

**John Garnett
Director,
The Industrial
Society, 1962–1986**

Top tip

When you're assessing who could do the task, consider what training or development they might need before you decide to delegate.

How to approach delegation

Case study

Rukia makes a SMART request in her one-to-one with Maria:

'We need to assess the effectiveness of our youth work in order to satisfy the terms of our grant.

'If we compare the number of beneficiaries we've served over a three-year period we should be able show our funder what we have achieved and therefore be eligible for further funding to extend our work. As the grant year ends in December I'd like the figures finished before the end of November. Are you able to take this on?'

The most important thing you need to remember at this stage is that you are making a request of a staff member. A request is a question about the possibility of doing things differently in the future. The best requests are SMART – **S**pecific, **M**easurable, **A**chievable, **R**ealistic and **T**imeframed.

The individual can respond to your SMART request in one of three ways. You must make it clear that all three answers will be respected.

1　Yes, I accept– 'I promise to deliver X by Y to Z standards.'

2　No, I decline. (For the possibility of a 'yes' to a delegation request to exist, the possibility of a 'no' must logically exist.)

There may be many reasons why someone would not feel able to take on an extra responsibility at a point in time, not the least of them being to do with life outside work.

It is a manager's duty to discover and understand the reasons for someone saying 'no'. But if the reasons are valid you have no choice but to accept 'no' for an answer. The alternative is for staff to feel that they have no choice but to agree to a delegation request because they fear that a refusal will be held against them. This does not engender an atmosphere of trust and probably will ensure that delegated duties are not carried out with enthusiasm.

A negative response on one occasion does not mean that every delegation request will be met with the same response. Individuals' circumstances change both at work and at home. Do not limit delegation possibilities on the basis of previous refusals.

3   A counter request from the staff member to negotiate the SMART terms attached to your request. For example:

'Can I commit to thinking about this overnight and come back to you in the morning ...' or

'Could I leave this until next month when my responsibilities for the Christmas Fair will be out of the way?'

A wise response is to agree to any counter requests. A willing delegatee is worth far more in motivational terms than an unwilling one and a staff member whose terms have been accepted is likely to be far more willing than one whose requests have been ignored.

Clarifying the objectives, policies and limits of authority

Once you have decided who you are delegating to and the individual member of staff has agreed, it is time to clarify the objectives of the job being delegated, any policies surrounding the task and the limits of authority for the person undertaking the duty for the first time.

In the following case study, Sarah explains the objectives of the task clearly. She outlines what Peter is authorised to do and reminds him of the expenses policy. She shows confidence in Peter doing a first class job, expresses her own availability if needed and agrees to notify the rest of the department as to what he will be doing.

Top tip

A twist on the SMART principle is to make it SMARTER!

Ethical – are you delegating a task just to 'pass the buck' or will it be a genuine opportunity for self-development for the person to whom you are delegating?

Recorded – write down exactly what the task is, when it needs to be completed and what the success criteria will be for completion.

Jamie Wilcox, Chief Executive, Volunteer Centre Kensington and Chelsea

Case study

Sarah: I'm not happy with our absenteeism situation – I think we need to look into it. I'd like you to do a survey of the last three years for me.

Peter: I've never done that on my own before. What's the best approach?

Sarah: It's up to you really. I'll let you decide how best to present the data. That said, I do want you to be clear on the objectives and what you are authorised to do. Your objective is to carry out a survey of all sickness absences less than seven days in the last three years. I want you to compare and contrast the data for each of our centres. Make sure you don't include any names of individual staff or managers … Is that clear so far?

Peter: We haven't all the data on computer. We only computerised the records last year.

Sarah: Oh yes. Of course. If you need to travel to any of the centres to get the data, you can claim back the expenses. Just check the staff handbook to make sure you stay within the guidelines. It shouldn't come to more than £200. Is that all OK?

Peter: Yep, fine.

Sarah: I want this be your number one priority. Do you think you could get it done and have the report in my hand by the end of June?

Peter: Sure. How will everyone know I'm not available until then?

Sarah: Don't worry. I'll send round an email. Oh, and Peter, I'm sure you'll do a great job on this, but if there's anything you need help with, just ask.

It is important for you to notify other people who will be affected, especially those in other departments whose cooperation may be needed by the individual in order to achieve the task. A simple memo or email will suffice.

An alternative approach, and a more personal one, is to take the person around to meet everyone who needs to know that he or she is doing the job.

Delegated responsibilities are best put in writing to avoid the possibility of misunderstandings. A simple format is shown in the case study on the next page.

Case study: A delegation plan

Name: Paula Harman (PH)	Task delegated by John Richards (JMR): Recruitment of staff		Target date: 1st October
Section of task	Additional authority needed	Additional training	Others to be notified
1 Designing and placing advertisements	Per advert: up to £500 online; £5,000 press; 20% of salary for recruitment agencies Total annual limit as per budget	A. Course on job advertising, June B. PH to draft all job advertisements for next month, JMR to coach	MG
2 Shortlisting for interview		A. PH to spend three days with heads of departments B. PH to redesign all application forms as a result of A	BR, AWB, MWT, FJB
3 Initial interviews		Course on interviewing, July	
4 Use of aptitude tests	Access to organisation-wide test results database	PH to be coached by JMR. Self-sufficient by July	
5 Letters of appointment	To be prepared by PH and signed by JMR	PH to study employment protection legislation and visit SPL for tips	SPL

Top tip

When setting a deadline for a delegated task, don't expect the person to whom you are delegating to take the initiative of coming to you if there are problems. They may not do so, especially if they feel confused and are too embarrassed to admit it.

**Mike Phillips,
Freelance Trainer
and Consultant**

In the case study, John Richards, the manager, should not forget to make the necessary adjustments to the job descriptions of both individuals involved. Staff recruitment should be removed from his own and added to Paula Harman's job description.

Review dates

Once you have set a deadline for a delegated task, set some review dates. The first should be quite soon after the task is set, so that the person you have delegated to can bring up any questions they may have about the task.

Regular review dates will ensure that you will not get any nasty surprises at the last minute or find that a task has either not been completed or has not been completed in the way that is required.

Chapter 3

The process of delegation

This chapter looks at the stages of delegation and conducting spot checks.

The five steps

> *'By the inch, it's a cinch. By the yard, it's hard.'*
> *Old saying*

There are five steps in the delegation process that are best undertaken gradually to ensure complete understanding.

First stage

- The manager does the job in question.
- The staff member observes and asks questions.

Second stage

- The manager briefs the staff member and allows time for questions.
- The staff member does the job under the guidance of the manager.
- The staff member comments on their own performance and the manager coaches and comments.

Top tip

If the individual already feels overloaded, find ways to help them review priorities and stop doing things that are relatively unimportant. This will create the space for them to feel able to accept delegated tasks.

Mike Hudson, Founder and Director, Compass Partnership

Third stage

- The manager briefs the staff member and leaves.
- The staff member does the job with no guidance but is allowed to ask for advice if it is needed.
- The staff member reports back on success or otherwise.

Fourth stage

- The manager hands over the job to the staff member.
- The staff member does the job in the absence of the manager.
- The facility to report back is at the discretion of the new jobholder.

Fifth stage

- The new jobholder takes over full responsibility for the task.
- The manager reserves the right to do spot checks.

Spot checks

Delegation does not mean abdication. Even when mistakes are not being made in delegated jobs, the manager still has the accountability for performance. This means that some system of control has to be devised. The spot check is the simplest method. If the task involves liaison with another department or team you can have a quiet word with your counterpart and ask how they see the employee's handing of the new task. If the delegated duty involves running a committee, you can ask the committee members for their views. If the job requires a written report, you can ask to see it.

The spot checks should be occasional rather than regular. They have to be enough to ensure that everything is being done to the right standard but

Top tip

Once the task is delegated and you've been coaching and supporting the individual, remain interested but do not be tempted to interfere unnecessarily or take over.

Top tip

Consider your volunteers when delegating – they may have skills and experience outside the organisation which would make them perfect for the task.

Jill Thornton, Personnel Coordinator, DSC

infrequent enough to show the staff member that you trust them to do the job.

A good manager will praise their team member when they are doing a good job. This can be done publicly or privately and is best done face to face. A close second is a handwritten note that shows you have thought about what you want to say, rather than an email that can be dashed off in seconds. A delegated job being done well deserves to be recognised.

Management by exception

The task has been handed over to the individual and you have the confidence that it is being done well. You have carried out a number of spot checks and nothing is awry. What happens then?

Rely on management by exception. Assume that the accepted standards are being met unless you are told otherwise. The adage 'No news is good news' applies in this situation.

You should ask for any reports to highlight deviations from the norm, both good and bad, rather than contain all the detail of the performance of every task. Good managers rely on deviations being reported to them, rather than having to search through masses of details to find them.

Where next?

Real Delegation, JK Smart, Prentice Hall, 2002.

Chapter 4

Coaching delegated staff

This chapter looks at the skills of coaching – an essential part of any delegation process.

Coaching skills

Coaching is now recognised as one of the key approaches to developing engaged and responsible employees and to helping them improve their day-to-day performance at work. It is also a great way of encouraging people to think creatively for themselves, and so is a crucial aspect of effective delegation.

Every conversation about a delegated task has the potential to become a coaching conversation and yet it would not be appropriate for every conversation to be the same. There are times when a manager needs to tell individuals who are carrying out delegated duties where they are going wrong or what is expected of them, and there are other times when a manager's aim should be to get a staff member to think a problem through for themselves. Both approaches are aimed at producing a performance shift and are coaching conversations.

There is a spectrum of coaching skills that embraces both extremes:

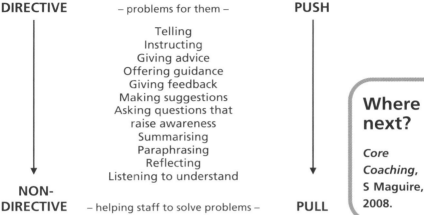

DIRECTIVE   – problems for them –   **PUSH**

Telling
Instructing
Giving advice
Offering guidance
Giving feedback
Making suggestions
Asking questions that
raise awareness
Summarising
Paraphrasing
Reflecting
Listening to understand

NON-DIRECTIVE   – helping staff to solve problems –   **PULL**

Where next?

Core Coaching, S Maguire, DSC, 2008.

Effective managers understand the whole of the spectrum and know how to use all of it.

When to be directive (push)

- **When you need to transmit facts and information that only you possess.** In this situation the necessary communication should be clear and unambiguous.
- **When you need to explain quickly why a change is needed and what it should achieve.**

When to be non-directive (pull)

- **When you both have the time and feel the need to get a staff member to think things through.** You can delegate more effectively by giving a member of staff the chance to take responsibility for coming up with their own ideas. By asking something like 'how do you think we could make this work?' you can encourage them to do so. This independence means that the individual is more likely to become committed to and enthusiastic about doing the job.

Where next?

Coaching for Performance, J Whitmore, Nicholas Brealey, 2009.

This approach builds the staff member's confidence, knowledge and self-reliance and so increases the capacity of the organisation.

A simple structure for a coaching conversation is the GROW model

A good coaching conversation about a delegated task contains the following elements:

Goal – what the coachee wants to achieve from the conversation.

Reality – achieving understanding of the current position: who, what or how much has the coachee already tried?

Options – what the coachee believes might be possible and what options there are for achieving the goal.

Wrap-up – what decision has been made and which actions will be taken. Is the task clear and is the coachee committed to and supported in doing it?

If there is no outcome it has been a chat, not a coaching conversation.

Key questions to ask are:

- What would you like to get out of this conversation?
- Ideally, what would you like to happen?
- What might or could you do?
- What stops you?
- What will you do?
- When do you think you can complete the task?
- On a scale of 1 to 10 how certain are you that you can do this?
- What would increase that from an 8 to a 10?

Top tip

'Socrates believed it possible to help people to understand but not to make people understand.'

Max Landsberg, author – *The Tao of Coaching*

Good managers challenge generalisations. The more you can help the other person to be clear about exactly what is happening right now, the more options the member of staff is likely to be able to generate.

If the staff member cannot suggest any options at all try asking:

'What would it be like if you could wave a magic wand and put everything right?'

As a general rule a manager moves towards the non-directive (pull) end of the spectrum by asking questions rather than making statements. For example:

'We can't finance that' might become:
'How could we finance that?'

In a coaching conversation you do not have to accept every suggestion from the staff member, however keen the other person is to try it. A good manager knows that there are occasions when judgement is needed. They can distinguish between their own caution and discomfort with a suggestion from a staff member and a genuine business objection. If it is the latter, explain the issue and ask how it might be included or addressed.

Effective managers use the whole of the spectrum depending on what response each occasion demands, and they find more occasions to be non-directive rather than merely telling staff what is required.

Top tip

Do not ask 'why?'. 'Why' is always followed by 'because': it creates defensiveness, justifications and closes down options. You can always turn 'why?' into 'what?', 'when?' or 'how?'

Margaret Lloyd, coach and author, Walking with Leaders

Where next?

The Tao of Coaching, M Landsberg, Profile Business, 2003.

Chapter 5

Feedback and evaluation

The final chapter looks at how to give feedback on the individual's performance.

The purpose of feedback is to help a person perceive the effect of their behaviour. It enables them to make decisions about how they may change their behaviour in future.

The two-step approach

There is a two-step approach to giving feedback.

1   What I thought you did well . . .
2   My suggestions for future improvements are . . .

Avoid linking 1 and 2 with 'but', 'though' or 'however'. Such linking words destroy the impact of the positive feedback.

How to give feedback

When giving feedback you need to:

- obtain permission to give it
- be clear for whose benefit it is
- get the time (as soon after the event as is sensitively possible) and place right
- be specific, using facts and examples. If you use opinions they need to be stated as opinions

> **Top tip**
>
> Feedback is a mirror which I can use to help me to see how I appear to others and the impact my behaviour is having on them. It enables me to identify facets of my behaviour, which I may choose to change.
>
> **Anne Stratton, Graduate Development Manager, Bentley Motors**

- state why the feedback is being given
- focus on doable changes
- focus on behaviour, not personality
- check that your feedback has been received in the way it was intended.

Handling mistakes

Delegation involves calculated risk and in spite of careful preparation sometimes you will find that an employee has made a mistake when working on a delegated task. How you should react will depend on the reason for the mistake.

A failure to consult

If the staff member didn't consult someone, either internally or externally, and irritated that person as a result, you will need to check whether you made it sufficiently clear who was to be consulted. If the lack of consultation resulted from your error, you should apologise to the irritated party. If it was clear who should have been consulted but the staff member overlooked it, then they must make peace with the offended person. In this situation highlight the importance of inter-departmental cooperation to your team member.

A lack of planning

If a staff member makes a mess of a delegated job through a lack of planning, some patient coaching would probably pay off. They may have assumed, from watching you, that the job was easy because years of experience made the planning process seem almost automatic. Coaching the staff member to use a step-by-step planning process should help.

A lack of confidence

Sometimes a delegated task will grind to a halt because the staff member lacks confidence. This may be because

Top tip

When giving feedback and identifying strengths and weaknesses, try to keep the ratio 2:1, positive:negative.

Heather Brierley, Training Consultant, DSC

Where next?

DSC runs several management and self-development courses. See www.dsc.org.uk/ Training for more information.

the task requires a public speaking presentation, chairing a meeting or using a database that they have never tried before. Whatever the reason for the lack of confidence, the answer will probably lie in more coaching to discover the reason in question and then the necessary training to overcome it.

Failing to measure up to the delegated task

In this situation you must use your judgement. Is it better to give more time to training the individual? Or is it better to cut your losses and take back the delegated task or give it to another staff member? Only by using your judgement can you decide. The important thing to remember in this situation is that decisiveness will breed respect and that indecisiveness will breed the opposite. Being decisive doesn't mean that the situation should not be handled with sensitivity.

Evaluating a delegated task

Evaluating the results of delegation is easily overlooked. If you have delegated a task successfully, you have a good opportunity to learn from the exercise. It is worth asking yourself a few questions.

- Has the staff member found new ways of doing the job that can be copied elsewhere?
- Is the individual concerned capable of further development?
- Are there other managerial jobs that could be delegated?
- Has the exercise motivated others in the department to seek more responsibility?
- Can anything be learned from the training needed to perform this sort of task?
- How much of your time has actually been saved?
- Can you improve your coaching skills further?

Evaluating a successful delegation exercise will reassure a manager that good delegation does definitely pay.

Top tip

While analysing delegation mistakes, keep two things firmly in your mind. First, the truism that everyone makes some mistakes some of the time and second, that mistakes are opportunities to learn.

Where next?

Managing Without Profit, M Hudson, DSC, 2008.